Letting God Lead

21 Day Transformational Leadership Devotional

John M. Kennedy

Letting God Lead

21 day transformational leadership devotional

John M. Kennedy

Letting God Lead Copyright © 2018 by John M. Kennedy

All rights reserved. Printed in the United States of America. No part of this book may be used or reproduced in any manner whatsoever without written permission except in the case of brief quotations em- bodied in critical articles or reviews.

Book and Cover design by Eric Little, Lilson Graphics

First Edition: October 2018

ISBN: 9781728909059

10 9 8 7 6 5 4 3 2 1

FORWARD

Today prayer and meditation are crucial to the growth and development of one's spiritual journey. Pastor John Kennedy, in this riveting 21-day Devotional, captures the essence of what is needed to do just that. This is a limitless work of art that will challenge its readers to focus, grow and strive for excellence!

Apostle Michael L. Favors
Pastor, Empowerment Action Center
Marietta GA

CONTENTS

INTRODUCTION 1

ONE 3

TWO 6

THREE 9

FOUR 12

FIVE 15

SIX 18

EIGHT 25

NINE 28

TEN 30

ELEVEN 33

TWELVE 36

THIRTEEN 39

FOURTEEN 42

FIFTHTEEN 45

SIXTEEN 49

SEVENTEEN 52

EIGHTEEN 56

NINETEEN 59

TWENTY 62

TWENTYONE 65

INTRODUCTION

The Christian leaders' life is generally led by a different set of rules and guidelines. Ive found so often that the Christian leader would be expected to lead like world leaders, who are pushed to please the people and give them what they want. Their lives are motivated by something other than the will of God. This could be challenging for some of us. As we come to learn the purpose and the person of God, we see that life isn't truly about us. To please a God that gave of Himself for you and me. It is here that we find the difference between world leadership and Kingdom leadership. Although we find many of the same qualities in both types of leaders the one thing that sets us/them apart is the willingness to please God over money and self.

Letting God Lead

It is often said that it takes 21 days to start a habit and each habit starts with an act today you just started your road to a better you in Christ. I would title this book act like a leader, but God would'nt want us to act He'd tell us to BE and leader.

DAY 1

Covenant
cannot be conditional.

"Abide in Me, and I in you. As the branch cannot bear fruit of itself, unless it abides in the vine, neither can you, unless you abide in Me. I am the vine, you are the branches. He who abides in Me, and I in him, bears much fruit; for without Me you can do nothing." **John 15:4-5 (NKJV)**

The umbilical cord forms five weeks after conception and is considered one of the major "supply-lines" for a baby. It's the connection between the mother and child that is essential for the supplying of oxygen and nutrients to the baby and the expulsion of its waste. Many complications with the umbilical cord can result in the underdevelopment of a child and even cause death.

Letting God Lead

Therefore, this connection is crucial to the success of the baby's proper development.

Much like the umbilical cord, is our connection with Christ and those chosen by Him to walk with us. Our connection is called covenant, and without it, we are not able to accomplish anything successfully, whether it be great or small. Our continued and consistent connection is crucial. Any complications or breaches in our covenant (unforgiveness, jealousy, contentions, gossip, etc.) will result in developmental defects and death within our ministries, families, and lives. That is why is it is vital that we stay continually connected to God for direction and one another for the fulfillment of purpose - no matter what.

> ➢ *Lord, help us to stay connected in covenant to You and those you have specifically chosen to walk alongside us.*

Letting God Lead

> *Help us also, to be mindful of any complications that may be forming or has formed within our covenant connections, so that we can take immediate action to correct them. IN CHRIST JESUS NAME, AMEN!*

Reflection Questions

1. Who do I turn to God first for guidance? (Proverbs 3:5-6)
2. Is my immediate response to adversity, trust in God or fear?
3. How do I nurture my relationship with God?

<u>Closing Affirmation:</u> I will stay in consistent communication with You Father and allow you Lead me throughout my day!

DAY 2

God
revealed IS resurrection.

"Jesus said to her, 'I am the resurrection and the life. He who believes in Me, though he may die, he shall live." **John 11:25 (NKJV)**

When Winter comes, the underparts of trees and plants survive the cold and remain alive, by resting and living off food that has been stored up. However, the upper portions die until Spring returns and life is revived. This natural life cycle is very similar to our spiritual life cycle. Through the process of growth and maturation we experience in Christ, we often find ourselves having to face "Winter" moments. Whether it be a "death" in relationships, habits, preconceived notions, or even our socio-economic status. This season of downsizing will come. But remember that this is not a complete death, just death to certain things. The key is to have enough food stored up so that you can survive until Spring returns and life is renewed. We as followers of Christ must consistently "gather" from God and His word if we could ever hope to be sustained through our coming Winters.

> **Lord, help us to be disciplined and intentional in our gathering times with You so that we will have much food stored up to sustain us and give us rest until our Spring returns. IN CHRIST JESUS NAME, AMEN!**

Reflection Questions?

1. What do you believe about Jesus today?
2. Are you willing to try Jesus in a different; way that you may know him different?
3. Have you found Jesus to be more to you than what has carried you over in your dry seasons?

Closing Affirmation: I will stand in faith despite life's trials and tribulations; I trust that you are with me and I will live.

DAY 3

To receive God,
we must expect Him. To expect Him, we must know Him.

"But without faith it is impossible to please Him, for he who comes to God must believe that He is, and that He is a rewarder of those who diligently seek Him." **Hebrews 11:6 (NKJV)**

Depending on the type of bird, the parent may visit the nest between 10-100 times daily for a single feeding session, and each time the nestling can be heard screeching in anticipation for what they are expecting to consume. Baby Robins are born with their eyes shut and remain this way for five days post their hatching. During this time, they begin to recognize in stages who their parents are. First, they distinguish them by the vibration they feel from the side of the nest as the parents arrive for feeding.

Then they become familiar with the shadow their parents cast in the sun. By the time the fifth day has come, and their eyes have fully opened, they already know the voice of their parents.

Isn't this just like our developing relationship with God through Christ? In the beginning, we are but babes, blind to who God is and the knowledge of His purpose for our lives. But over time through consistent prayer, the study of his word, fellowship with Him and time spent in His presence through the glory of His Son; our eyes become open. We can now recognize him in His existence and His voice. We are finally able to see clearly that all we will ever need and expect can only be found in Him.

- **Lord, help us to remember that You are our expectation and if we purpose ourselves to know You in the pardon of our sins and fellowship with Christ; we will never lack anything we need or cease to obtain direction in what we are seeking. IN CHRIST JESUS NAME, AMEN!**

Letting God Lead

Reflection Questions?

1: Do you find it difficult to be consistent in seeking God for daily advice and guidance?

2: Have you experienced growth in your walk with God? Assess this by the time amount of time you spend devoted to prayer and study of His word.

<u>Closing Affirmation:</u> Today, my work will speak for my maturity in God: as my time with Him has developed, so has my standards and the things that I do.

DAY 4

You must believe
in the power of God residing in yourself; God sees you differently.

"But you are a chosen generation, a royal priesthood, a holy nation, His own special people, that you may proclaim the praises of Him who called you out of darkness into His marvelous light." **1 Peter 2:9 (NKJV)**

Moses, Jeremiah, and Gideon all had objections to the call that God placed on their lives. Each was attempting to reveal to God some flaw that He made in their design. God doesn't see us according to our perception of what is acceptable and correct. God sees us in His image because that is how He made us. Therefore; not only do we already look the part, but we are already more than capable to do all things through Christ Jesus.

Letting God Lead

> ➤ **Lord, remind us that we are a reflection and extension of You on this earth and with that blessing comes everything we need to do Your will in excellence. Lord, sever us from the spirit of fear and help us to remember that You have already endowed us with a high level of grace, eloquence, and skill to bring about a great victory. IN CHRIST JESUS NAME, AMEN.**

Reflection Questions?

1: How many times did God have to show you that you're bigger and better than you think you are?

2: When was the last time God asked you to do something you felt was bigger than your money or knowledge?

3: Could it be we still see ourselves in the Image of the crowd God pulled us from?

John M. Kennedy

Closing Affirmation: Today I choose to see myself the way you see me; by walking with those you called me too not with those you called me from.

DAY 5

Don't buck the system,
surrender to it.

"Trust in the Lord with all your heart and lean not on your own understanding; In all your ways acknowledge Him, And He shall direct your paths. Do not be wise in your own eyes; Fear the Lord and depart from evil. It will be health to your flesh, And strength to your bones." **Proverbs 3:5-8 (NKJV)**

Have you ever met someone who refuses to read the directions before assembling a product? They usually end up leaving an important piece out or become so frustrated that the project remains incomplete indefinitely. These things happen when we try to walk out our Salvation without the Holy Spirit and the people God places in our lives to stir us along the way. We often choose to "lean to our own understanding" by relying on our understanding and perceptions regarding a matter - sometimes it seems morally sound or because it brought good results in the past. In doing so, we fail to realize that we are not acknowledging God in all our ways. This type of behavior will always cause us to enter repeated cycles of errors, dormancy, stagnancy, and frustration.

> **Father, please help us to be consistent in pursuing You through the Holy Spirit. We acknowledge that He is available to us so that we can always be on the right track in our daily walk with Christ. Help us not to be deceived in believing we can ever be wise on our own. We recognize that we will always "buck" without You. IN CHRIST JESUS NAME, AMEN!**

Letting God Lead

Reflection Questions?

1: Are you done trying to do life without God?

2: How many times will we miss the mark and keep moving forward as if it didn't matter?

Closing Affirmation: Today, I'm done doing it without God's guidance. I will take my time and do it right, rather than rush and do it half-hearted or with out instructions.

DAY 6

Love is a lifestyle!

"Love suffers long and is kind; love does not envy; love does not parade itself, is not puffed up; does not behave rudely, does not seek its own, is not provoked, thinks no evil; does not rejoice in iniquity, but rejoices in the truth; 7 bears all things, believes all things, hopes all things, endures all things. Love never fails. But whether there are prophecies, they will fail; whether there are tongues, they will cease; whether there is knowledge, it will vanish away." **I Corinthians 13:4-8 (NKJV)**

Merriam Webster's dictionary defines love as: "a feeling of strong and constant affection for a person." Dictionary.com defines feeling as: "a belief…" and defines constant as: "a situation or state of affairs that does not change." Therefore, love must be a strong belief that does not change. Right? God's love for us is called Agape, meaning its perfect in its expression, strength, and constancy.

Letting God Lead

We love to say that "We Love Like Christ" but the minute someone "gets on your nerves", the very first thing being cross examined is love. But God's love for us has NEVER changed. Why? Because true love never fails and He meant it when He said it. Not only that, He sent his son, Jesus Christ to show us how to love strongly and constantly even when others have not earned it. Jesus giving His life on the cross helps us to see that true love forgives and transcends offense no matter how many times an injustice is committed. Love should NEVER be put on trial.

> - **Lord, help us to love as Jesus has taught us to love. Help us to forgive, as Jesus has taught us to forgive. Help us to learn how to truly "LIVE LIKE CHRIST" by living a life that "LOVES LIKE CHRIST." IN CHRIST JESUS NAME, AMEN!**

Reflection Questions?

1: If someone described how you loved them: what would it sound like what would they say?

2: When you show love, what does it look like afterward: is it loud and boastful or puffed up and paraded?

3: What are some of the best examples we can take from Jesus showing us how he loved?

Closing Affirmation: Father God, today help my love language sound like you. Please give me the ability to love like Christ.

Letting God Lead

DAY 7

Stop waiting for people to validate your dream. It was VALID as soon as God gave it to you! #DreamBig

"Then the word of the Lord came to me, saying: Before I formed you in the womb I knew you; Before you were born I sanctified you; I ordained you a prophet to the nations.'

Do not say, 'I am a youth,' For you shall go to all to whom I send you, and whatever I command you, you shall speak. Do not be afraid of their faces, for I am with you to deliver you,' says the Lord.

Then the Lord put forth His hand and touched my mouth, and the Lord said to me: 'Behold, I have put My words in your mouth. See, I have this day set you over the nations and over the kingdoms, to root out and to pull down, to destroy and to throw down, to build and to plant.'" Jeremiah 1:4-5, 7-8, 9-10 (NKJV)

Every year a man by the name of Mitch Matthews hosts an event called The Big Dream Gathering. During this event, hundreds come together to learn how important it is to dream again and keep on dreaming. Before it begins, his staff hangs several signs around the venue that will later serve as categories for dream posting. Once Mitch releases the participants to dream, they each obtain a dream number that they write at the top of their dream sheets.

Participants can write as many dreams as they can dream and then hang them under the proper category (education, relationships, spiritual, family, etc.). After this is done, the participants can walk around and view other dreams to write motivational comments of encouragement or even advice to help push the author of that dream closer to their goal. In the end, Mitch has the participants collect their dream sheets, and he releases them to walk out their dreams. God has already done this for us through His Word, hasn't he?

Letting God Lead

He tells us in Habakkuk, that if we would just take the time to write our visions (dreams) down in a readable, well thought out format so it will be easy to understand and implement. God further tells us in Jeremiah that we do not need to be concerned about the how's of what seems impossible to us because He is with us and He has put His own words in our mouths. God has strategically endowed us with the ability to do greater works. We have been pre-selected and pre-established to see our dreams become a reality. Remember, our seemingly impossible dreams are a direct reflection of God's will for us.

> **Lord, Our God, let us once again see the value in our dreams. Help us to navigate through and bypass our restrictions. Help us to rely on what You've said and not what "they" may or may not say. Lord, help us to continue to #DreamBIG and keep on dreaming. IN CHRIST JESUS NAME, AMEN!**

Reflection Questions?

1: How hard is it at times for you to believe that God has already blessed and ordained you for a great work?

2: Do you still remember when God put the dream in you to do the things your doing today? Did you feel it was easy or hard for you?

3: Did you find it easy to write it down and share with others?

Closing Affirmation: Today I believe that I am exactly what God said I am and I will do everything that He has ordained for me to do.

Letting God Lead

DAY 8

Worshipers don't quit, workers do!

"So, the Lord spoke to Moses face to face, as a man speaks to his friend. And he would return to the camp, but his servant Joshua the son of Nun, a young man, did not depart from the tabernacle." **Exodus 33:11 (NKJV)**

There is nothing worse than waiting all day for a delivery and nothing comes. But as soon as you leave your home, the delivery arrives. Most times, due to the nature of the delivery, it will be returned to the warehouse, and you will end up having to submit a request to have it delivered again.

Have you ever wondered how many "deliveries" the Angels return to God because we've left His presence too soon?

Ever wondered how much sooner you could've received that answer, directive or deliverance you've been anticipating? If only we'd sat a little longer or pressed in a little further, perhaps what we hoped and expected would already be ours. Joshua recognized that just because the priest leaves, doesn't mean God's presence is gone. He waited, and one day he received both a promotion and the mantle.

> **Lord, help us NOT to become so busy that we are missing pivotal moments at Your feet. Help us to understand that the creatures (employer, family/friends, leaders) in our lives are not our source; but You, our creator is. Help us to realize that our call to worship is not a career move or busy work that we can just walk away from as our flesh dictates. But to love and value You, is to worship You daily in a consistent and thorough way - in season and out of season. IN CHRIST JESUS NAME, AMEN!**

Letting God Lead

Reflection Questions?

1: Could you pass the wait test? The stay here until I return test? Joshua's ability to wait on God and his leader was seen all through his life.

For example, Mose on the mountain telling him to stay here until he returns for 40 days.

2: Is what I'm waiting for worth the wait?

3: Have you ever turned away from something man gave you to manage?

Closing Affirmation: Father, today I will no longer get out of place or get a head of you. I will wait on the Holy Spirit.

DAY 9

God's Word is always the best counselor.

*"Your word is a lamp to my feet and a light to my path." **Psalm 119:105 (NKJV)***

There is so much help that awaits us in God's word. It doesn't matter how a problem or dilemma may present itself; there is a scripture to clarify, direct and heal us. Jesus sent His Spirit to "lead and guide us into all truth." But what is His truth? Well, if Jesus is truly 'the way, the truth, and the life", He is also the word that was made flesh. God's word is also His truth; and His truth (word), will make us free in mind, body, and spirit. We can only receive all the benefits of God's counsel when we read the word.

Letting God Lead

➢ **Lord, Your word is indeed a lamp to our feet and light to our path. Help us to discipline ourselves in reading and studying Your word so that we can see better in every area of our lives. IN CHRIST JESUS NAME, AMEN!**

Reflection Questions?

1: Are you still in love with reading Gods word as you were when you first met the lord?

2: How much has the word of God changed your life today?

<u>Closing Affirmation:</u> I will commit to reading and turning to God'S word more and more for the plans for my life.

DAY 10

Elevate your expectation beyond what you know.

"Now to Him who is able to do exceedingly abundantly above all that we ask or think, according to the power that works in us." **Ephesians 3:20 (NKJV)**

The world thought it was advancing when dot matrix printers were developed, but I believe the world let out a sigh of relief when LaserJet printers were invented. Technology has advanced by leaps and bounds over the years by adding new features that allow us to print, scan, fax and copy. But who knew that one day, we'd be able to print in 3-D form? This newest technology is a phenomenon made for sci-fi movies. But all it took was a moment of imagination, and an "I wonder if...?" in elevated thinking to bring those blueprints to life.

"I wonder if...?" is the type of mustard seed faith that God wants us to have in expectation of Him. Start asking yourself: "Is God Able?"- YES! "Is God Capable?"- YES "Is God Willing?"- YES! I believe that once you realize that God can, God wants to, and God is willing to; ABSOLUTELY NOTHING WILL BE IMPOSSIBLE TO YOU!!!

> **Lord, please elevate our thinking about You and our expectation of You. Let what we believe become compatible at the level of who You are. Help us not to perceive you according to our earthly limitations. Help us to realize that You have an unlimited number of ways in**

> **which to accomplish one thing for us. Help us to remember that creating the impossible is just one of the things You do best! IN CHRIST JESUS NAME, AMEN!**

Reflection Questions?

1: Are you still think your last big idea was the best you could come up with?

2: Are you willing to rethink and make changes to the idea or solution you last came up with that worked.

3: Would you know if your season was up or old?

Closing Affirmation: I will dream again. New ideas will come to me again. I will finish well.

Letting God Lead

DAY 11

You are NOT supposed to carry the weight of this life, but to carry the weight of HIS people.

"…casting all your care upon Him, for He cares for you."
I Peter 5:7 (NKJV)

"Bear ye one another's burdens, and so fulfil the law of Christ."
Galations 6:2 (NKJV)

God in His wisdom and strategy divinely connects us with people who can help us better maneuver through this life. When He made Adam, He made it clear that man should not be alone and that He would provide a "help meet" for him.

A helpmeet is someone compatible to you and thereby able to help you by meeting you where you are in life. Sometimes we go through trials and tribulations not knowing exactly why, but when we cast these troubling things at The Lord's feet, we find that we can overcome them. Then, later in life, we meet someone who is entering the same season we have victoriously exited. Through our testimonies and experiences, we can meet people where they are, and better help them to become triumphant as well. For this reason, Peter 4:12-13 encourages us to "think it not strange when we go through..." and to "count it all joy."

- **Father help us to be better help meets or accountability partners to one another for your Kingdom. Help us to trust You enough to handle our burdens as we humble ourselves to bear the issues of our brothers and sisters. IN CHRIST JESUS NAME, AMEN!**

Letting God Lead

Reflection Questions?

1: When was the last time you carried a problem by yourself that God had someone around to help you with?

2: How many days did you go to sleep with the wait of the world on you that you should have given to God?

3: Do you really believe in your purpose and your own testimony?

Closing Affirmation: I will. I can. I was made to help to walk along side my brothers, sisters and love ones.

John M. Kennedy

DAY 12

When God gives you a break; take advantage of it.

"He makes me to lie down in green pastures; He leads me beside the still waters. He restores my soul…" **Psalms 23:2-3 (NKJV)**

Stress is often referred to as a silent killer. Why? Because you may never know you are stressed until it's too late. It can have a very negative effect on your body and can cause anything from high blood pressure to strokes and heart attacks. The body was never made to handle stress at the magnitude we allow and when we try to do it all at the expense of our health; sometimes death is our reward.

Letting God Lead

But God has promised to give us rest "beside the still waters," reset us as He "restores our soul" and provides for us as we "lie down in green pastures."

> ➢ **Lord, help us to recognize the breaks that You give to us. Help us not to fill every free moment with another obligation, when You are blessing us with the space to rest. Help us to realize that we are not You and You are the only one who can do all things and never stretch yourself thin. Thank you for your attentiveness towards us. IN CHRIST JESUS NAME, AMEN!**

Reflection Questions?

1. Spend some time thinking about rest and how much you get?

2. How healthy are you mentally, emotionally and physically?

3. Are you the type of person who bites off more than they can chew?

Closing Affirmation: Father God, today when you give me time; I will take some of it and do nothing but rest!!

Letting God Lead

DAY 13

Do something to get God's attention!

"And He said, 'Do not lay your hand on the lad, or do anything to him; for now I know that you fear God, since you have not withheld your son, your only son, from Me. Then the Angel of the Lord called to Abraham a second time out of heaven, and said:

'By Myself I have sworn, says the Lord, because you have done this thing, and have not withheld your son, your only son — blessing I will bless you, and multiplying I will multiply your descendants as the stars of the heaven and as the sand which is on the seashore; and your descendants shall possess the gate of their enemies. In your seed all the nations of the earth shall be blessed, because you have obeyed My voice." **Genesis 22:12, 15-18 (NKJV)**

Wow! What an amazing response from The Lord! From a biblical standpoint, the term obedience means to hear, to listen, to reverence, to comply and to submit. What better way to get God's attention than by living and operating in a level of obedience that lets Him know that who He is and what He says means much more to us than what He does.

> **Our Father who art in heaven, hallowed be Your name. Your Kingdom come. Your will be done on earth as *it is* in heaven. Give us this day our daily bread..." (Matthew 6:9-11). Then Lord, please help us to bring an offering of obedience before you every day. IN CHRIST JESUS NAME, AMEN!**

Letting God Lead

Reflection Questions?

1: When was the last time you believe God asked you to give up something that you loved dearly out of obedience?

2: Are there some things that God might have been testing about your faith; we didn't hear his voice to stop but we let it go anyway/or killed it?

3: Have you loved anything in your life more than the obedience to your God?

Closing Affirmation: Today I believe my obedience is the key to the blessings and the open doors that God has for my life. I will move according to what I hear him say.

DAY 14

There is no covenant without the blood!

"And as they were eating, Jesus took bread, blessed and broke it, and gave it to the disciples and said, "Take, eat; this is My body. Then He took the cup, and gave thanks, and gave it to them, saying, drink from it, all of you. For this is My blood of the new covenant, which is shed for many for the remission of sins." Matthew 26:26-28 (NKJV)

WA covenant is a binding agreement. In the Old Testament, it was instituted between God and Abraham's descendants, primarily to teach His people how to operate in obedience and submission by using animal sacrifice. The last and final covenant was between Jesus Christ and man - "Whosoever will…" (Mark 8:34), that offered us a freedom of relationship with God through direct access via prayer, confession, and true repentance. Both covenants required the shedding of blood, but only one included a "lamb" that God Himself sacrificed to give.

> **Lord, help us to value the blood and sacrifice that our covenant through Christ required. Help us not to allow sin and tradition to negate the sanctity of this new covenant. Remind us that the blood Jesus shed at Calvary still works to wash and keep us and will never lose its power! IN CHRIST JESUS NAME, AMEN!**

Reflection Questions?

1: Do you still find communion Sunday to be important in your life.

2: Do you view it as you and God making an agreement?

3: Are there any covenant agreements you made with God that you need to repent from and move on in a stronger commitment with him?

Closing Affirmation: Today I will be true to my word and obedient to yours, Father God. I will not break covenant on this walk with you again.

Letting God Lead

DAY 15

If you are not growing, you are not in covenant.

"I am the true vine, and my Father is the husbandman. Every branch in me that beareth not fruit he taketh away: and every branch that beareth fruit, he purgethit, that it may bring forth more fruit. Now ye are clean through the word which I have spoken unto you. Abide in me, and I in you. As the branch cannot bear fruit of itself, except it abide in the vine; no more can ye, except ye abide in me.

I am the vine, ye are the branches: He that abideth in me, and I in him, the same bringeth forth much fruit: for without me ye can do nothing. If a man abide not in me, he is cast forth as a branch, and is withered; and men gather them, and cast them into the fire, and they are burned. If ye abide in me, and my words abide in you, ye shall ask what ye will, and it shall be done unto you. Herein is my Father glorified, that ye bear much fruit; so shall ye be my disciples. **John 15:1-8** *(NKJV)*

If you break a branch from an apple tree, it will not bear fruit any longer. It will instead die. Likewise, if we disconnect ourselves from Christ, then we too will begin to see things die in our lives and will find that we have ceased to bear good fruit. Our constant connection to God through our relationship with Christ is imperative. Depending on the level of relationship we have in Christ, even the slightest disconnect could prove detrimental. This point was proven when Moses lost his opportunity to go into the promised land because he allowed people to cause him to disobey God's command. (Numbers 20:7-12)

> **Lord, You said that as long as we remain connected in covenant with You, we can expect to bear good fruit. But, you also said that if we are not connected and not bearing good fruit, then we will be removed from you**

Letting God Lead

> ➢ and cast away. Lord, help us to be obedient to You and the Holy Spirit so that we are not counted amongst those branches who are deemed fruitless, useless and therefore bound for the fire. IN CHRIST JESUS NAME, AMEN!

Reflection Questions?

1. How often do you keep dead things in your life that are not bearing fruit. Is it because you like it that you let it stay around?

2. Could it be that your plans aren't working because you took God and his word out of the plan?

3. Who are you letting hang around that's causing you to disobey God? Is it worth not having the promises the blessings that He has for you?

John M. Kennedy

Closing Affirmation: Today, I will walk by faith. I will finish my course. I will keep the faith. I will bear much fruit today. I choose to live and not die.

Letting God Lead

DAY 16

Bring Jesus your little, so it can be multiplied.

"A certain woman of the wives of the sons of the prophets cried out to Elisha, saying, "Your servant my husband is dead, and you know that your servant feared the Lord. And the creditor is coming to take my two sons to be his slaves." So Elisha said to her, "What shall I do for you? Tell me, what do you have in the house?" And she said, "Your maidservant has nothing in the house but a jar of oil."

Then he said, "Go, borrow vessels from everywhere, from all your neighbors—empty vessels; do not gather just a few. And when you have come in, you shall shut the door behind you and your sons; then pour it into all those vessels, andset aside the full ones. So she went from him and shut the door behind her and her sons, who brought the vessels to her; and she poured it out.

Now it came to pass, when the vessels were full, that she said to her son, "Bring me another vessel." And he said to her, "There is not another vessel." So the oil ceased. [7] Then she came and told the man of God. And he said, "Go, sell the oil and pay your debt; and you and your sons live on the rest."
II Kings 4:1-7 *(NKJV)*

During those times when you find yourself destitute and unsure what your step will be, remember this amazing testimony of God's ability to work in multiplicity! The scripture tells us about a woman who felt destitute and feared that the little she had would be the end for her and her son. BUT GOD! Through her trust in the Lord to make good use of her "little," He not only multiplied what she had to cancel her debt but more than enough for her and her son to live off the rest.

Letting God Lead

> **Lord, our Lord, how excellent is Your name in all the earth! Just like the widow, we can cry out to You and know that You will listen. Lord, we also believe we can trust You with our "little" and You will not fail to provide for us. Thank You for being true to Your word! IN CHRIST JESUS NAME, AMEN!**

Reflection Questions?

1: Do you truly believe that the smallest thing, the least in your house could truly be the breakthrough or answer that God wants to use for your worst situation?

<u>**Closing Affirmation:**</u> I believe that what's in my hand you can and will use? Today, what I have right now is more than enough for my breakthrough to come.

DAY 17

Tell God "Thank you."

"…give thanks in all circumstances; for this is God's will for you in Christ Jesus." **I Thessalonians 5:18 (NIV)**

It's important throughout our life to make sure we thank God not only when things are going well, but through the hard times when we think we need Him the most. When transitions happen, it's imperative to remain flexible; to keep an attitude of gratitude and a posture of praise on your lips. Paul is an excellent example that teaches us to stay thankful because we learned of ALL the hardships he suffered for Christ's sake.

Letting God Lead

We aren't thanking God for the bad things per se, but we are thanking God in ALL things. Take a moment to think about where you could have been, the life you could have had, the life you currently have and simply say, "Thank you." This becomes a testimony of the glass being half full; optimism saves us every single time. God works out everything for the good of those who love Him. He will never leave you or forsake you. You are never alone.

At the end of the day, God gave his only son to die for our ratchet selves and even on the cross he loved us enough to carry our burdens! The least we can do is be grateful. It's time for us to grow up and make being gracious a commonality amongst ourselves. Let's give Him thanks just because He's God and He's worthy.

> Father, thank you. Thank you for reminding us we are not deserving but you loved us enough anyway to carry us through our circumstance. We appreciate your loving kindness towards us day after day. We now realize there is nothing we should have to complain or murmur about because You and You alone carry us – one step at a time. We commit to be being a better steward over our graciousness to you. In Christ Jesus Name, AMEN!

Reflection Questions?

1: Have you been complaining about things not happening fast enough or going your way? If so, why?

Letting God Lead

2. When people come to you with their problems; are you an encourager or do you join the pity party with them?

3. Do you believe that you're suffering, or hardships are necessary for your growth and true fellowship with Christ and his afflictions?

Closing Affirmation: Today I will not complain, I choose to have praise and thanksgiving on my lips; for God is still good to me.

John M. Kennedy

DAY 18

I am doing a NEW thing.

This is what the Lord says - he who made a way through the sea, a path through the mighty waters, who drew out the chariots and horses, the army and reinforcements together, and they lay there, never to rise again, extinguished, snuffed out like a wick: "Forget the former things; do not dwell on the past.
See, I am doing a new thing! Now it springs up; do you not perceive it? I am making a way in the wilderness and streams in the wasteland. There are times in our lives when we can become complacent to the NEW thing and we wind up missing His will for our life. **Isaiah 43:16-19**

Sometimes we fail to miss how powerful and mighty the Lord, our God is. As a people we want to harbor the things of old, but yesterday is gone and we cannot get it

Letting God Lead

back. We must let go of yesterday, let today take care of itself and will tomorrow presents itself we deal with it when it comes! Tomorrow presents a new day – a new opportunity for us to get it right. As Papa will always fulfill his promises to us, we can rest assured that our journey begins anew.

> **Lord, thank you for sending new! Help us to release the old yesterday so we can move into Your promises for our life. Lord God Almighty, lead us into what's next for our life and not be settled for what we have already accomplished. We ask for it all in your power. IN JESUS NAME, AMEN!**

Reflection Questions?

1. Have you downloaded the things God is doing in your life today?

2. Do you remember the things God did for you yesterday and the day before that?

3. Can you let go of what's behind you and believe for greater promises that are in front of you?

<u>Closing Affirmation:</u> I'm choosing right now to let go of the former things and press toward the mark of the prize set before me; I will move into my new now.

Letting God Lead

DAY 19

There's <u>no</u> competition in the Kingdom.

There are different kinds of gifts, but the same Spirit distributes them. There are different kinds of service, but the same Lord. There are different kinds of working, but in all of them and in everyone it is the same God at work.
1 Corinthians 12:4-6

Think back to that one time when you really wanted a gift so badly and walked up to some person and almost demanded that's what you wanted. Once you received the gift, you were beside yourself with joy. Now take a moment to weigh the adverse effect. What if you received the same gift but your attitude toward the same gift was nonchalant and lackluster. How do you think the person you received the gift from would feel?

I believe this is how God feels when he brings us gifts and we don't use them to edify and advance the Kingdom. The Lord blessed His people with many gifts and talents. How do you think He feels when you don't learn your gifting or use it to its full potential? God doesn't create clones. Each one of us are special – fearfully and wonderfully made. Our goal is to learn and exercise the gift God we were gift so we are empowered to do the work of the ministry.

> **Father God, thank you for showing us we are different by design. Holy Spirit, reveal our gifts and teach us how to use our gifts so windows of opportunity are availed to us. IN JESUS NAME, AMEN!**

Letting God Lead

Reflection Questions?

1. Have you allowed the free gift of God to give you the big head and think more highly of yourself then you should?

2. Has there been a time you saw someone operating in their gift and you wanted their's more than the one you had?

3. Do you really know what gift God has given you today?

<u>Closing Affirmation:</u>

Father God today I will use my gift and allow my gift to make room for me. I shall walk in the open doors you have for me.

DAY 20

I will grow in my Faith.

So then, just as you received Christ Jesus as Lord, continue to live in him, rooted and built up in him, strengthened in the faith as you were taught, and overflowing with thankfulness.
Colossians 2:6-7

In today's society, we want things done quick, fast and in a hurry. As a result, we find ourselves in a position of frustration because it isn't happening at rapid speed. Growth is a process. If we wanted to plant a garden, we first must prepare the soil, then we apply the seeds, give them sunshine and rain and eventually we will begin to see buds. For growth to be successful, we must do the work, we must remain faithful, available, teachable, flexible and most importantly, willing to apply what we learn. If we do these things, we will grow in faith while growing closer in our relationship with Christ.

- ➢ **Father give me the patience to wait. Empower me to walk in Your ability to live according to Your plan for my life. I thank you in advance for seeing me better than I see myself and giving me strength to want to be better than I am. IN JESUS NAME, AMEN!**

Reflection Questions?

1: Have you been taught the value of growing faith with patience?

2: How many stages in your Christian faith have you skipped by wanting everything now?

3: When did the rate of growth cause you to waver in your faith? What is you planned response for that going forward?

4: Do you know what process of life you're in right now?

Closing Affirmation:

Today I choose to take time to grow in God, to study my Word, and pray.

Letting God Lead

DAY 21

I will model generosity.

One person gives freely, yet gains even more; another withholds unduly, but comes to poverty. A generous person will prosper; whoever refreshes others will be refreshed. People curse the one who hoards grain, but they pray God's blessing on the one who is willing to sell.

Whoever seeks good finds favor, but evil comes to one who searches for it. Those who trust in their riches will fall, but the righteous will thrive like a green leaf. **Proverbs 11:24-28**

As children of the Most High, our goal is to give just like Christ has given to us time and time again. Although we can't beat God's giving; we must be conduits of forgiveness, blessings and opportunity. Our job is to shareand provide service to those in need.

By being generous like our Father, we find ourselves without lack.

> **Father God, thank you for teaching us this lesson of reaping and sowing. The more we give, the more you give to us and we are forever thankful. There isn't a day, minute, or an hour that goes by that I am not affected by your level of giving! Bless my heart so I continue to give more generously. IN JESUS NAME, AMEN!**

Reflection Questions?

1: Has giving become a priority in your life as a believer?

2: Have you received anything from God that you didn't feel you deserved or that you didn't even ask for?

3: Do you give freely or do you find yourself feeling obligated to give?

Closing Affirmation:

Today I choose to give out of the abundance of my heart for I am a cheerful giver.

John M. Kennedy

About the Author

Pastor John M. Kennedy has been an exemplar in ministry ledership for more than 20 years. Deeply rooted in evangelism, Pastor John has lead small groups, ministry teams, multiple ministry departments and since has been pastoring for the last 7 years.

He has also studied leadership at Beulah Heights Bible College. His love for God and passion for people, both saved and lost drives his ministry. He has trained many transformational leaders that are making a significant impact for the kingdom of God. Journey with him for 21 days to fortify, challenge and charge your ministry as a leader amongst leaders.

Made in the USA
Columbia, SC
19 August 2022